GOD CODE

DIVINE MATRIX

PROF. R V M CHOKKALINGAM

Copyright © Prof. R V M Chokkalingam
All Rights Reserved.

ISBN 979-888546457-4

This book has been published with all efforts taken to make the material error-free after the consent of the author. However, the author and the publisher do not assume and hereby disclaim any liability to any party for any loss, damage, or disruption caused by errors or omissions, whether such errors or omissions result from negligence, accident, or any other cause.

While every effort has been made to avoid any mistake or omission, this publication is being sold on the condition and understanding that neither the author nor the publishers or printers would be liable in any manner to any person by reason of any mistake or omission in this publication or for any action taken or omitted to be taken or advice rendered or accepted on the basis of this work. For any defect in printing or binding the publishers will be liable only to replace the defective copy by another copy of this work then available.

The book is dedicated to our family deity Sri Subrahmanya Swamy @ Kuppam.

Contents

About The Book

The book identifies, classifies, and analyses an interesting, but neglected arguments for the existence of God. The question of existence of God is ambiguous and hard to agree. The existence of God is a subject of debate in the philosophy of religion, and culture. There exists a set of evidence that we have not quite fully explored. An intricate code of God is hidden within the vast and infinite universe. Divine Matrix refers to the universal field of energy that connects everything. We must assume behind this force the existence of conscious and intelligent Mind. The God Code is real and the truth of divine creation is hidden in the Divine Matrix. Science has hinted at the existence of God by indirectly suggesting that the universe is still mysterious. The author attempts to explain the mysterious phenomenon of God through the chapters on Creator God, Consciousness, Dynamic Patterns, Intelligent Design, Unifying Principle, Polar Opposites, Fine-Tuning, Clockwork Universe, Cosmic Dance, and Conversing Universe. We humans need to understand that every person is made of the same stuff and made by the same Creator. The elegance of the laws of physics and the laws of mathematics has empirically proven the evidence of the Creator Deity. The teleological argument from design asserts that certain features of the universe and of living things must be the product of an intelligent cause. Religious experience and cultural belief in God has always been normative among humans and so people do not need to prove the existence of God. The proofs for the existence of God have always been presented in a fairly large probability though not absolute certainty. There must have been a time when nothing existed, so there must exist a Being with necessary existence regarded as God. Whatever begins to exist has a cause, the universe began to exist and therefore, the universe had a cause-God. Consistence revelations described in scriptures lead to belief in God. The universe is strongly analogous in its order and regularity similar to an artefact such as a watchmaker, and so the existence of the universe justifies the presumption of a divine creator of the universe-God. The secret God code of the universe, once unveiled will help us achieve the divine unity with the universe and ourselves. The personal witnesses both contemporary and throughout the ages, which rely on testimony of supernatural events establish the existence of God. Every human being has the God imprints literally imbedded in his or her DNA as well as in Fingerprints. The naturalistic evolution is incapable of providing humans with the cognitive apparatus necessary for their knowledge to have positive epitomic status, which is a divine attribute. There has to be a First Cause or that there is a necessary Being from whom all contingent beings derive their existence. We can see that there must have been an Unmoved Mover from our experience of motion in the Divine Matrix of the universe.

CHAPTER ONE

Creator God

It is relatively common place that the natural sciences, philosophy, and theology are great universe even had a beginning or an eternal past before the Big Bang. Science is understood as being concerned only with the tangible world, not the inner world of the subjective. Scientists inquire about the nature of objective reality without factoring in their own existence. Of course, scientific materialism divides the world into two domains: the objective and the subjective. The truths of the universe are written out there on the universe itself, and are accessible to us all through the process of inquiry. It appears that there is a vast, hidden wisdom, or structure or blueprint for even the most simple-looking element of nature. There is no more scientifically explicable than the mysterious ability of non-physical mathematical constructions to determine the workings of our physical world. Not in the least understood by science, who initiated the creation of our universe.

The fact that universe is comprehensible is a miracle. We see a universe marvellously arranged, obeying certain laws, but we do not know how deep we understand them. Science is an amazing, wonderful understanding: it teaches us about life, the world, and the universe. But does the vast knowledge base of science disprove the existence of some kind of pre-existent outside force that may have launched our universe on its way. But it has not revealed to us why the universe came into existence nor what precede its birth in the Big Bang. Scientists do not try to prove or disprove God's existence as there is no experiment that can ever detect God. Many people believe that he natural world, and humanity's existence in the universe point towards a Divine Creator that brought forth all of this existence. It may not be unnecessary to prove the existence of God in order for belief in God to be reasonable. The concept of God who transcends space and time, and gives existence to all things is the foundation of the shared worldview of all religions.

Science cannot prove the existence of God, but it cannot disprove God either. Scientists have yet to discover and fully understand the science that God built into the natural world. We are amazed at the phenomenal working model of the real thing- planets rotating on an axis and all revolving around the Sun. How is that we can look at the real thing and believe that it is a random-chance accident with no designer or creator. Biological evolution has not brought us the slightest understanding of how the first living organisms emerged from inanimate matter on this planet, and how the advanced life forms ever emerged from simpler organisms. If the fundamental laws of nature explain everything, then what explain those laws. Things did occur in a very specific way here on Earth. God of the gaps argument appeals to divine intervention to explain that might be explicable by purely physical rules alone. The emergence and continued existence of complex life in our universe is fragile and this triggers a genuine sense of wonder about creation that can ultimately point to God.

We have a faith that only serves to enhance and enrich us, but not take away the wonder of science. We need to make life from non-life, but this is no easy or small fact, which is one of the greatest puzzles around the natural scientists in all disciplines. The emergence of intelligent life is so outlandishly unexpected and our universe must have been designed specifically to give rise to us. The fundamental particles created in the Big Bang had the correct properties to enable the formation of substances which produced the stars. The physical laws governing the nuclear reactions in the stars then produced the stuff that our life is made of. How come all the physical laws and parameters in the universe happen to have the values that allowed stars, planets, and ultimately life to develop. We have not seen any evidence of the laws of physics ever being broken in the universe. If God exists in extra dimension, before cosmic inflation, or outside of space and time altogether, neither proof nor disproof is possible. There must have been a First Cause at a definite point in time.

It is no wonder that the universe as big as it is, for, it displays the power and majesty of God. The witness of signs and miracles are thought to herald the existence of God. How does the nature of the universe relate to the nature of God? God is central to many people's moral values, yet the existence or non-existence of God is often taken as an assumption rather than needing evidence itself. Is God's nature one of the inexplicable brute facts about the world? God is the most perfect being- a being greater than which none can be conceived- entails that God exists, Is there any way to understand why God has the nature? The fine-tuning of our universe is a positive argument about the intricate structure of the universe as a whole, and forms the evidence of God. Are ther a unique set of physical laws that govern the evolution of our universe into producing intelligent life? Several other arguments attempt to prove the existence of God, and also the argument from intelligent design. All worldly objects can change from potential to actuality, but the cause of that change must be something besides the object.

What would convince us that God exists? For the deeper, we delve into the mysteries of cosmos, the more the universe appears to be intricate and incredibly complex. The idea is to question what caused the Big Bang? The Big Bang burst of energy about 13.7 years ago, whose nature and source are completely unknown to us. If the cause is physical as per science, we have gone nowhere. If the cause is otherwise non-physical, it must be supernatural. Many argue that there must be ultimate cause or explanation for the existence of the universe and that it must be God, or the existence of a higher power. But physicists now investigate the most fundamental characteristics of nature and track issues that have long been the province of philosophers and theologians. Another argument is that God is not a good explanation because what would explain God? We do not know why the tiniest particles of matter are so unbelievably complicated. Why is our universe so precisely tailor-made for the emergence of life? This question has never been answered satisfactorily.

The eternal question- is there a god or is not there? How do we know that God exists? Of course there are those who categorically say there is no god. We call them atheists. Agnostics are those who are not sure if there is a god or not, since the creation of the world. People always believe in the almighty God, and that ever exists. For example we cannot see oxygen right, but somebody tells us it exists, and we believe it correct. There is no way we can prove God does exist or not. Why the nuclear fires inside stars, give us carbon, iron, nitrogen, oxygen, and all other elements that are so essential for life to emerge? Why the elemental charges set precisely to the exact level need to attract and capture electrons, which then begin to circle nuclei made of the protons and neutrons. How the highly complicated double-helix molecule, the life-propagating DNA would be formed? Why everything we need in order to exist come into being? How as all of this possible without some latent outside power to orchestrate the precise dance of elementary particles required for the creation of all the essentials of life?

Science and religion are two sides of the same deep human impulse to understand the world, to know our place in it, and to marvel at the wonder of life and infinite cosmos we are surrounded by. The belief that God became the universe is a theological doctrine that has been developed several times in human history. The incredible fine-tuning of the universe presents the most powerful argument for the existence of an imminent creative entity- we call God. We lack convincing scientific contrary, such a power may be necessary to force all the parameters needed for our existence. If two particles are entangled, we automatically manipulate its partner, when we manipulate it. Then how does this spooky action at a distance in quantum entanglement happen. All that requires a faith that God can multi-task, keeping the fabric of space and time in operation. The power of thunderstorm, the beauty of a flower, the intricacy of a snowflake, the majesty of snow-capped mountain, and the immensity of our vast universe- all declare the glory of God.

The quantum theory has revealed aspects of nature that seem supernatural: the act of observing something can apparently alter its reality. The clear focus of Genesis is that all of creation reflects the wisdom, power, and care of God. We cannot peer inside black holes or view anything that lies beyond the distance that light has travelled since the start of the Big Bang. Panpsychism sounds very much like what we call the Brahman, the tremendous universal Godhead of which we are all a part. Breathing is a miracle, which keeps us alive. Spiritual breathing is like physical breathing, which is a process of exhaling the impure, and inhaling the pure. We experience our own mind every waking second, but we can only infer the existence of other minds through indirect means. Natural selection instilled in us the capacity for a so called theory of mind- a talent for intuiting other's emotions and intentions. There seems a connection between the brain's bio-molecular processes and the basic structure of the universe.

The existence of God is the proposition that there is a supreme or supernatural Being that is the creator or sustainer or ruler of the universe and all things in it. The laws of the universe are identical to the collective consciousness, and they reveal an answer to every question we are capable of asking. God's algorithm is a notion that only omniscient being would know an optimal step from any given configuration. When we look at the workings of the universe right from quantum level to cosmic level, it seems apparent that there exists God algorithm, which we can hardly decode. The universe is a dynamic system with astounding precision that we cannot decipher the architecture of God's software. The divine beings are personification of the cosmic forces, vital to creation, sustenance, and recycling of existential order. God is the supreme or ultimate reality. Omnipotent, Omniscient, and Omnipresence is the description used by theologians to describe God's universal presence. In Hinduism, Brahman connotes the highest universal principle, the ultimate reality in the universe.

CHAPTER TWO

Consciousness

The non-physical aspect to human consciousness is held as indirect evidence of God. The supernatural character of the workings of human consciousness adds ground for raising the probability of the existence of a supernatural God. Working of human consciousness is miraculous as consciousness has no physical presence in the world, similar to the laws of mathematics. Thoughts and images in our consciousness have no measurable dimensions. Our non-physical thoughts, somehow, mysteriously guide the actions of our physical human bodies. All astonishing things that happen within the conscious workings of human minds, functioning outside physical reality, offers rational evidence that human beings may well be made in the image of God. If we are unconscious, we do not even know whether we are alive, or dead. If we are in deep sleep we are alive, but we do not know it. The only reason why we experience life and aliveness is because we are conscious. What we call consciousness is the basis of our life and our existence. Consciousness is a boundless dimension and limitless in nature.

The important characteristic of consciousness is the composite of all conscious awareness and conscious experience. How can physical atoms and molecules, for example, create something that exists in a separate domain that has no physical existence, namely human consciousness. There are two schools of thought: one holds that consciousness is part of the material structure of the universe, and the other holds that consciousness is merely an illusion generated by the activity of neurons. Another view is that consciousness resides in an as-yet unknown space in the universe. There is other popular approach that consciousness is merely a user illusion- a trick of the mind. We are conscious when we are the subjects of an experience. It becomes impossible to talk about consciousness of God if we cannot accept that consciousness is an actual, but immaterial entity. Consciousness is a non-material, non-physical state that basically has no beginning or ending. Consciousness exists potentially everywhere from the macro to the micro, when conditions are supporting of its manifestation in the physical realm.

As humans, we know, we are conscious because we experience and feel things. Consciousness is our inner experience of what things feel like. We are conscious and that is the understanding nature of reality. All we do know for certain is that we are having a conscious experience. It is the only thing we can objectively say is certain. It is the most inescapable fact without consciousness there is no reality, and without consciousness, we would not be aware of all the real stuff that is out there. Conscious experience is obviously a part of reality, without understanding how consciousness relates to the unknown physics, our understanding of the universe is incomplete. Without consciousness there is no reality. The question of how consciousness can acquire knowledge about the external world has a long history in philosophy. Some philosophers argue that consciousness as we think it is an illusion, and could be something extra-an additional ingredient in nature. The most certain and familiar phenomenon of consciousness obeys none of the usual rules of science.

We as a piece of body and as life are a certain amount of earth, water, air, fire, and ether. There is a fundamental intelligence that puts all these things together in a particular way to make life out of it. Some call this intelligence as consciousness that makes life happen. According to religious faith is that an all- powerful, supernatural entity created us. Panpsychism means that consciousness is the fundamental quality of nature. A fundamental theory of consciousness tries to weave consciousness into the fundamental fabric of reality, albeit in a very specific way. Some feel consciousness is a manifestation with a real, physical location, somewhere in the universe. Others think perhaps the heavenly body radiates out consciousness as our Sun radiates light and heat. Yet others suggest that consciousness is produced and transmitted through the quantum vacuum or empty space. The scientifically inexplicable and intractable character of human consciousness leaves behind the scientific materialism as a complex basis for understanding the world of human existence.

The scientifically unfathomable quality of human consciousness inhibited the very scholarly discussion of the subject in recent years. Scientists and philosophers have proposed countless contradictory hypotheses about what consciousness is and how it arises. One of science's most challenging problems is a question that can be stated easily: where does the consciousness come from? Scientists and great thinkers are unable to explain what consciousness is and they are equally baffled where it comes from.

Panpsychism claims that consciousness is inherent in even the tiniest pieces of matter-an idea that suggests the fundamental building blocks of reality have conscious experience. It implies that consciousness could be found throughout the universe. We do not know even that consciousness requires a brain at all. There is no particular reason to assume that consciousness occurs only in certain kinds of matter. On the other hand, we would not need to accept the strange claim that consciousness does not exist, while it is so obvious that it does.

Everything that we know or experience is through consciousness. There is nothing that we know more intimately than conscious experience, but there is nothing that is harder to explain. The hard problem of consciousness is the real problem of explaining why any physical state is conscious rather than unconscious. The role of emergence in the creation of consciousness has been debated for over a century, but remains unsolved. Why would the fact that we are conscious have anything to do with the ultimate, underlying nature of reality. Vedantic perspective tries to explain that consciousness is only one, singular, identifiable with its universal source-Brahman. Vedanta advocates the idea of subjective evolution of consciousness as the developing principle of the world. Every argument that we could possibly make, will be made from a perspective of conscious observation. Without consciousness no matter, how immensely intelligent we are, we will be just another kind of present day robot existing in this world without having the awareness and experience.

Consciousness is a subjective feeling, when we sit down and plan on something, there is a very logical process which translates those thoughts to paper. They seem to flow spontaneously from us through consciousness. Consciousness or perception originates in our brain drains of energy plateau in our neurons. Consciousness poses the most baffling problem in the science of mind. The hard problem of consciousness is the problem of explaining the relationship between physical phenomena such as brain processes and experiences. Consciousness is one of the very important functions of the mind and is even considered as the supreme mental function, because it makes sentient in a specific way and differentiates us from present day artificial intelligence. What if consciousness is not something special that the brain does, but is instead a quality inherent to all matter. We work with conscious paradigm and is fundamental to all there is. We need to understand the evolution of consciousness across many lives and many dimensions.

We do not know how consciousness, the brain, and the soul are intertwined. The nature of consciousness as suggested by the Eastern traditions is necessarily universal and primal. It is fundamental and manifests itself in the gradation form of all sentient and insentient nature. We know that consciousness is a force within the human body, and only when it is conscious it will stand up and perform its usual activities. The moment consciousness leaves, the body collapses. In a living body it is not just the molecules, bones, tissues, and so forth that are all in all, but the body has a foundation upon consciousness. The perceived spatial and temporal plurality of consciousness is merely an appearance or illusion. Consciousness is truly puzzling phenomenon. Our own consciousness is the only element of existence and we are personally aware of through the flow of subjective experience. We perceive an external reality and ourselves demarcated from it. Scientists have long been trying to understand human consciousness- the subjective stuff of thoughts and sensations.

Without consciousness nothing is experienced either here or out there. We are so used to assigning consciousness to human thought that it takes effort to see it as universal or cosmic applying at all levels. This is because the mind looks directly at itself rather than outward at things. The main characteristics of consciousness are joyfulness, a revelation of the meaning of purpose, and aliveness of the universe. Cosmic consciousness is perfect awareness of the oneness of life as the universe is filled with one life. In cosmic consciousness one becomes united with the universal knowledge and life. Cosmic consciousness is an inherent, natural faculty of all human beings. In cosmic consciousness, one observes that this universe is a living entity and finds oneself eternal as a soul. Since the universe is God and God is the universe, consciousness of cosmos means God realization. The mystery of consciousness leads us to the existence of God and for those who would like to believe in God, the mere existence of consciousness help their belief.

We humans have the body, which merely is a medium to be able to dwell here on earth. We return our body back to earth, but exist in our real form of soul without that of the earth body. When ejected from the body, the consciousness and creativity goes beyond the limitations of the earth sciences. Consciousness does not seem to be physical, cannot be observed except from within, cannot be really described, and does not abide by the laws of nature. It has been bequeathed to us by God. God is understood to be of infinite dimensions from the point of view of human consciousness. Higher consciousness is like a flash of insight with no connection to the understanding. Some of the world's most renowned scientists are questioning whether the cosmos has an inner life similar to our own. Modern science though shrinking the gap between human and the rest of the universe, it does not know where the consciousness come from. Physical science describes matter from the outside in terms of its behaviour. But matter from the inside in terms of intrinsic nature is constituted of consciousness.

CHAPTER THREE

Dynamic Patterns

The divine proportions existing in the smallest to the largest parts in living and also non-living things reveals the awesome handwork of God. There exists a divine proportion that is exhibited in multitudes of shapes, and patterns whose relationship can only be the result of God's scripture. The divine proportions of beauty, function, and order are an inherent part of these shapes and patterns found ubiquitous throughout creation. The divine proportions are ubiquitous in their presence throughout all of creation with their symmetry, beauty, and mathematical preciseness evident in every aspect. Their very presence is virtually everywhere and in everything. The rational conclusion seems that the Creator of the universe is intelligent being, and these things are a visible fingerprint of his invisible, yet personal existence. The Fibonacci pattern is one of God's marvellous mathematical wonder. It is also found in the spiral arrangement of leaves around a plant's stem, when viewed from above. The times of revolution of the planets around the Sun correlates with the arrangement as an amazing phenomenon.

The chambered nautilus is the clearest example, wherein it retains its identical form as the body of the organism grows in the path of a spiral that is equiangular and logarithmic. The beauty of this form never changed and is commonly called the Golden Spiral. The spiral is visible in things as diverse as galaxies, whirlpools, hurricanes, human ear, DNA molecule, sunflowers, daisies, dandelions, ram's horns, sea-horse tails, fern leaves, and tornados. The spiral inevitably follows a precise mathematical pattern. In sunflowers, we observe two sets of spirals with rows of seeds or florets spiralling in opposite directions, and these follow Fibonacci number sequence. This numbering pattern reveals itself in various ways throughout all of nature. We should realize that the information to produce these spirals and numbers in living things is stored in the DNA. The DNA molecule is literally one long stack of Golden Rectangles. Mathematics reveals patterns that reflect the orderly character of God. God has truly put his inspirational signature on the patterns of the universe.

Geometric patterns exist all around us, creating the fundamental structure and templates of life in the universe. It is said that every natural pattern of growth or movement comes back to one more geometric shapes. We are surrounded by a kaleidoscope of visual patterns- both living and non-living. By studying patterns in nature, we gain an appreciation and understanding of the world in which we live and how everything is connected. Patterns in nature thrive because they are part of a complex web of interrelationships. Nothing in nature happens without a reason, all of these patterns have an important reason to exist and also happen to be beautiful to watch. A fractal is a detailed pattern that looks at any scale and repeats itself over time. Snowflakes, trees branching, lightning and ferns are examples of fractals. A Voronoi pattern provides clues to nature's tendency to favour efficiency, the nearest neighbour, shortest path, and tightest fit. The examples are the skin of a giraffe, corn on the cob, honeycomb, foam bubbles, the cells in a leaf, and a head of garlic.

Devine patterns are sequences that are seen throughout the universe in math, science, nature and connects us with each other. We are in awe at the vastness of the universe and impossible aspects of space. Division of human body into half in length-wise, shows that this vertical axis would represent a mirror from which the image is the same distance as the reflection in it. It can be seen that we humans are created in perfect bilateral symmetry for balance. Man is made to walk on two feet, some to walk on all fours. and others to hop. The form of each creature lent itself to its mode of transportation, reproduction, identification, and survival. We can also see in mathematics that balance must be maintained between two sides of an equation. The universe maintains our metaphysical existence and humans are little bits of the Big Bang of a few billions ago. Modern physics proves that the whole perceived universe is made of vibrations. Every living organism vibrates and is in fact a wave phenomenon, a sinusoid that has a specific frequency, and amplitude.

Stars have patterns and most of the astrologers believe that our destiny depends on the patterns of the stars. We all together are star dust, waiting to retrace back into the universe. The universe is a cosmos because the phenomena of nature embody geometrical form and proportion. Every single atom inside of us is connected to some way, shape, or form to the rest of the universe we move through creation. The bodies of humans are proportional consistently with the Fibonacci sequence. The measurement of our human body from the navel to the floor and from the top of the head to the navel is in the golden proportion. Everything in nature is an evidence of mathematical relationships. Mathematics is discovered rather than invented, which has the power to reflect the essential nature of reality. There is an established order in the universe with scientific laws governing all things. There are orderly patterns in nature, which we can call laws in its properties, measurements, timings, and lives. The cosmos exists in a great harmony for it obeys laws which are divinely perfect.

There is ample evidence that the universe is one harmonious system. The key to understanding this harmony is by seeing unity in everything of divine proportions. Even the formation of natural forces and our planet follow the divine pattern like formation of mountains, waterfalls, canyons, and salt-flats. The human mouth and nose are proportioned at golden section of the distance between the eyes and the bottom of the chin. The shape and form of each living being is to fit it for the role it has to play. Life patterns build each of our own realities and lead each of us to our own true life's purpose. Mathematical relationships are shown in ideas of number, form, design, and symmetry, and in the laws governing the existence of all things. We see unique number sequence in the universal patterns, which are cues from the universe itself. To be able to perceive the absolute meaning of even one form, would have to mean perceiving the divine plan in its totality. It is the unity and harmony in the universe that allows the parts to function together as an integrated whole.

The golden ratio is sometimes called the divine proportion, because of the frequency in the natural world. All the patterns in the universe show us that there is a gap between the human beings and the universe, and that mathematics is the language that bridges the gap. It looks that mathematics is the alphabet with which God has written the universe. The patterns are the reminders of the miracles it took to make us exist. We live in an orderly universe of purpose, not an accidental one. Humanity is a microcosm, a reflection of the entire world-order in miniature. The law of divine oneness states that we are all connected through creation. Physicists have stumbled in signs that the cosmos is custom-built for life and consciousness. As belief can find inspiration in science, so scientists can find inspiration in belief. The correspondence between a model and pattern can be seen in the relationship between an algebraic equation and its corresponding geometric shape. The universe is indeed all powerful, and everything is acting within the rules of existence.

Divine Matrix is our universe and that is also everything in our universe, which connects everything in our lives and the universe. Divine matrix is a universal field of energy that connects everything in creation. The universe is part of us and we are part of the universe. The sacred part is a belief that all patterns, their mathematical formulas, and their structures are evidence of divine creation. Sacred Geometry looks at patterns that repeat in the universe as evidence of the building blocks of existence. God is the Mind of the universe and the whole we see as well as the whole we do not see. God is the ground of being, creativity, and energy. There is an interconnection between the universe and nature with harmony and proportion. Proportion is the comparison of sizes, harmony is the relationship of measures, and geometry is the function of numbers. The description of God is based on the real properties of the universe. When theists worship God, they unknowingly worship the cosmos. Numbers and qualities such as polarity, harmony, and proportion are archetypal principles of physical manifestation.

A Divine Force just sets up a little system that shows us a beautiful mathematical art and fascinating proportion. There is an invisible mechanism within the universe, and an Intelligent Mind is directing the mechanism. All the movements are measured, their events are plotted, and their creatures are developed with a well-defined objective. We can never say it is mere chance that our earth rotates around the Sun without the evidence of intelligence here. The infinite power of God works unseen, but manifestations appear in the effect. Creationists believe that the world was created and developed according to some preordained plan. Such a theory requires the existence of a Creator who is super-intelligent and all powerful. It becomes more obvious that the longer we live, all life is full of patterns. Science goes into the innermost depths of the atom and finds the entire universe is constructed from it. Everything around us and every event that happens to us is an expression of God. The energy out of which the universe is made is everywhere inseparable from our thought.

From a single molecule to a dancing galaxy, there is a logic, a measuring, and an unfolding pattern to it all. Everything in the universe is being carried on according to the pattern and the rhythm set by the Divine Power. Mathematics reveals patterns that reflect the orderly character of God. Sacred geometric patterns exist all around us, which are the perfect shapes and patterns that form the fundamental templates for life in the universe. Sacred patterns and shapes also represent the intangible, mystical elements of life. We see many animals have stripes or patterns for the purpose of camouflage. People look in the universe and search for patterns to reveal their real characters and destiny. Seasons have patterns as they come and go. Technology is the man's attempt at mimicking God's design. Mathematics is the alphabet with which God has written the universe. The universe is God's creative project, filled with beauty, pattern, and meaning. We could divine nature's secret patterns which have elegance, order, and power.

CHAPTER FOUR

Intelligent Design

Theory of intelligent design simply says that certain features of the universe and of living things are best explained by intelligent cause, not an undirected process such as natural selection. It is a new faith-based creationism alternative to evolution. Intelligent design theory begins with empirical observations from the natural world. It observes through experience that various structures are always made by intelligence. Intelligent design theory makes a testable prediction from observations from the natural world. Intelligent design theory is the claim that some features of organisms are so complex that they could not possibly have come into existence through normal causes, and hence demand the supposition of a designer who thought them up and them into place. It finds irreducible complexity and structures in biology are designed. There must have been an intelligence behind such a process. Life is put together in bits and pieces by a process. It starts with one process, then extend it, then modify it and so forth, until it reaches the state of things today.

Intelligent design theory claims that the irreducible complex adaptations found in nature is made by intelligent designer. It feels that the full understanding of the organic world demands the invocation of some force beyond nature- a force which is purposeful or at least purpose creating. Intelligence design theory says that intelligent causes are necessary to explain the complex, information-rich structures of biology and theses causes are empirically detectable. Irreducible complexity is defined as a single system which is composed of several well-matched interacting parts that contribute to the basic function, wherein the removal of any one of the parts causes the system to effectively cease functioning. An eye is not a useful system unless all its parts are present and functioning at the same time. It is impossible for complex patterns to be developed through random processes. The anthropic principle of Intelligence design states that the world and the universe are fine-tuned to allow for life on earth. The intelligence theory sees the appearance of design which pervades in nature as evidence for the existence of God.

Intelligence design believes that matter, the various forms of life, and the world were created by a designing intelligence. The chance of a world such as ours occurring without intelligent design becomes more and more remote as we learn of its wonders. The aspects of nature that exhibit specified complexity patterns that contain information and are too complex to have been formed simply by accident. The most famous specific instance of design offered by intelligent design proponents is the complexity of the machinery found inside cells. The universe, and some of the objects that compose it, including both living and non-living, exhibits abundant evidence of having been designed. Intelligent design is the belief that an intelligent creator is the cause of the universe, and this creator can be detected in nature. When we examine the complexity of life, the universe, the earth, and everything that defines existence is not the result of random chance, but is only possible through the work of divine intelligent creator.

The world contains order, regularity, purpose, and beauty. We see purpose everywhere that leads to assume the existence of purposive agents that have designed the world. Cells in our body communicate information with other cells by releasing and receiving various proteins. DNA is an instructional message that dictates how cells behave and this message is written in a special language that utilizes a unique alphabet. This special design could not logically come from natural evolutionary forces. It could only be produced of design from beyond any human intelligence. Human eye is often used as an example of an irreducible complex system, as per the theory of intelligent design. Intelligent design asserts that the combination of nerves, sensory cells, muscles, and lens tissue in the eye could only have been designed . It is a wonder to see eye like a top-of-the line modern camera that contains a self-adjusting aperture, an automatic focus system, and an inner surface that minimizes the scattering of stray light. The human eye is often cited as a perfect example of intelligent design.

Natural theology aims to demonstrate the existence of God and to establish the principal divine attributes to vindicate God's creation. The teleological arguments across cultures form design is developed for the existence of God. By looking at an object containing the properties of beauty, purpose, regularity, and order, we may infer that it was designed and the designer is called God. Stoic philosophers dismiss the atomistic idea that chance collisions of atoms formed the material. The design argument attempts to prove God through the concept of design. Many organized structures in living organisms- the elegant form and protective covering of the coiled nautilus, the interdependent parts of the vertebrate eye. the interlocking bones, muscles, and feathers of bird wings give the appearance of having been designed for a purpose. Living things often exhibit teleology, and products of chance do not. The universe is composed of energy, matter, time, and space. It is organized into durable systems that are sustained by immutable sets of governing principles.

God reveals his existence to everyone through nature. His intelligence, power, and creativity can be observed in every corner of the universe. Dolphins appear to be able to produce their own signature whistle, quite reliably. Most obvious form of communication that dolphins use is vocal signals referred to as frequency modulated sounds. Intelligent design holds that there are tell-tale features of living systems and the universe that are best explained by a designing intelligence. God's presence resides in his creations for us to experience. This includes the tiniest microbes, and fast moving galaxies in space. Many structures in plants and animals bear unmistakable signature of design by a supernatural intelligence. Natural teleology is concerned with empirical observation and reason, and its methodology overlaps to some extent with that of the natural sciences. Nature does not randomly generate instructional message, but they generate from a Mind that wants to convey specific information to intended recipients. The celestial features and the veracity of cosmic descriptions evidence the existence of God..

Design is a factor of intelligence in which God devised a plan for birds to accomplish the purpose of overcoming gravity in air. The bird's structure has been made of special material that is light enough to fly. It has a mechanism for its motion to happen freely. Birds have a distinctive outer covering with feathers attached to the bones essential for flight. Feathers overlap each other so that thickening is always on the leading edge of the wing to make the airfoil for lift. The feather has a Velcro kind mechanism to achieve this function of flexibility and strength with very little weight in order to make it effective for flight. The centre part of the feather is a vertical hollow shaft. There are many more unique features of bird feathers such as the wide variety of colours and patterns. Birds are some of the most prolific and diverse creatures on earth who also have the amazing ability to fly. The appearance of design in nature such as complexity, order, purposefulness, and functionality of living organisms can only be explained by the existence of a designer-God.

Nature displays purpose as birds have wings to fly and planets orbit in regular motion. In fact, Watchmaker analogy if we find a watch on a heath, we would assume that it has some designer, which we could say the same with nature. As with a watch, the attributes of purpose and regularity are suggestive of a designer- God. The components of a system could not have materialized from nothing, aligned themselves intelligently and then self-regulated harmoniously. Intelligent design theory detects design through theological reasoning that goes beyond what science itself can do. Intelligent design theorists argue that design can be inferred by studying the informational properties of natural objects to determine if they bear the type of information that in our experience arise from an intelligent cause. The teleological argument builds on an implicit and explicit analogy between created artefacts and the natural world. It observes the features of our environment exhibit orderliness and goal-directedness. Natural teleological arguments depend on the presence of God.

Intelligent design is a fine-tuning of nature that is just right for life. Natural process is undetectably guided in a natural-appearing way by a supernatural agent for the purpose of producing a particular natural-appearing result or design-directed action by a supernatural agent. The appearance of goal-directed complexity is far better explained by design than by mindless chance. DNA functions like a software program that arises from an intelligent source. Natural theology is the process of deriving knowledge of God from the use of natural human reason. In other words, it is an attempt to provide arguments for the existence of God on reason and ordinary experience of nature. No universe of this complexity could have come by sheer chance: some intelligence lies behind it. To formulate an accurate worldview, we must acknowledge the existence of God in all his fullness. We can make a conclusion that it came from outside source who is much smarter than we are which can only br described as God. It endorses theists realism affirming that God is objectively real.

The physical laws and constants are determined in a non-random manner by an external intelligence not bound by physical law. Intelligent design incorporates the known laws and constants of the universe and tries ties them together in a uniform theory to explain why they are coordinated to produce life-friendly physical parameters. We do not yet know the most fundamental laws and we cannot work out all the consequences of the laws we know. Anthropic principle shows that a power outside of space and time has had something to do with life on earth.

Intelligent design focuses on complex patterns by a Mind that conceives and executes a plan. Intelligent design is supported by a vast body of evidence ranging from physics, cosmology, biochemistry, to systems biology. The very mathematical elegance of the universe is also a compelling observation. The thumb print is an evidence of the existence of God because each person has an individual and unique thumb print. If we are to see the hand of the designer anywhere, it would be in the fundamental principles, the final laws of nature.

CHAPTER FIVE

Unifying Principle

There have been philosophers who observed the universe as a unified whole within which all things exist are subsumed. Particles and forces may converge at the most fundamental level either through radical physics like the superstring or through hidden particles like grand unification. With the view such as 'As above so below' or 'As within so without', patterns are contained within patterns, complete in and of themselves and different only in the scale. The universe has been designed by a Super Being in such a way that the whole arrangement has been set up to exploit the relations between the different parts. Our minds do grasp mathematics, mathematics does apply to the world, and mind and matter interact in manifold ways. Our universe is is a unified one that encompasses many functioning on totality. The parts of the universe fit harmoniously together with the possibility of a utilitarian calculus. We all speak in philosophically, scientifically, and spiritually about an indivisible unity –God dwells in us and the spirit living within our body fashions everything.

Spirituality has often reached the same conclusion through intuition that the universe is unified. Our universe is full of reminder of the beauty of interdependence reflecting the nature of God. The interconnectedness is how species within an ecosystem relate to each other both qualitatively and quantitatively. Nothing in the world stands by itself. Every object is a link in an endless chain and is thus connected with all the other. The life of the universe and its history lies in an infinite web of connections. The basic forms of connection may be classified as spatial, temporal, causal, and consequential. The materiality of the world conditions the connections of everything with everything else, expressed in the philosophical principle of universal connection. The universal interconnectedness of the elements within the whole at any level form essential condition for the dynamic balance systems. The human individual is not a lone traveller amid the jungles of existence. He is a part of the world interacting in various ways with the world.

Cosmological observations strongly support that there exists a deeper and fundamental connection and unity in the universe. Everything that happens in the world may be attributed to the interaction of things, one element of which is equilibrium. All forces are different manifestations of a single grand unified force. We can imagine our universe as a triangle with mathematics at the apex, and mind and matter at the two base angles. The universe constitutes a higher unity, and that its parts do not sit idly to produce results not obtainable otherwise. Every atom in our body comes from a distant star. We may spend our entire staring out at the world through a distorting lens. A beautiful image of natural fractals with self similar patterns remind us of the handiwork of an Almighty. The theory of Brahman focuses on all inclusive living. The interconnected universe has been gradually revealed objectively through math and science as well as subjectively through theology. It is difficult for an individual human being with the feeling of separateness to comprehend that everything is interconnected.

The central texts of the Upanishads contain the message of the unity of the mind and the world. The unified theory of physics is the theory of everything to explain fully cosmology, dark energy, dark matter, quantum mechanics, force fields etc. The architect of our universe created a world of embodied minds and knowable mathematical order. The universe qualifies as a organic unity, working as a unified whole. Quantum theory also suggests that everything is interconnected. According to Hindu concept the unified field is fundamentally a field of consciousness as the unified field constitutes the deeper reality and hence the true identity of everything in nature. Particles can also be thought as waves meaning that particles can exist in different states. Particles having no definite position, and being present in more than one position at the same time suggests a unity in everything. In physics a field is an area under the influence of some force, such as gravity or electromagnetism. A field theory refers generally to why physical phenomena happen, and how these phenomena interact with nature.

Strange events that defy normal scientific explanation point to a mysterious and strong interconnectedness of the universe. We have still questions that are unanswered. What is the nature of the mysterious dark matter and dark energy that make up roughly 95 percent of the universe? Why is there more matter than antimatter? The existence of Super God as only a designer like this can account for the organic structure present in the universe. Electromagnetism refers to interaction that affects electrically charged particles. Strong interaction is the force that binds together neutrons and protons into a nucleus inside the atom. Gravitational interaction is the attractive interaction that affects all bits of the universe, whether large or small, while undiscovered, the theoretical particle for the force would be the graviton. Scientists now struggle to mesh the subatomic and universal realm under one Grand Unified Theory. The Grand Unified theory is an attempt to understand the nature of matter, energy, space, and time.

The universe is metaphysically unified in such a way that the various parts of the universe whether of the same stuff or not are interrelated in such a way that an organic whole is the outcome. Timeless philosophies suggest the interconnectedness of all life and remind us of instinctive orientation toward unity. The metaphysical structure of life is interconnected, interrelated, and interdependence because it is irreplaceable. All lives are connected to one another in the stream of a large life. We human beings are part of the whole universe and a part limited in time and space. We are connected to the nature and dependent on it for things we need to keep us alive. All of the materials that constitute our bodies return to the matrix of life. Unity of life is crucial for everyone as unity is the law of existence and the purpose of life. The most important characteristic of the Eastern worldview is the awareness of the unity and mutual interrelation of all things and events. Scripture tell us in many ways that it is through the gift of the Spirit that God is the animator of all living things.

The Divine Matrix is the container that holds the universe and forms as bridge between all the things, To tap the force of the universe we need to see ourselves as part of the world, rather than separate from it. The focus of our awareness becomes the reality of our world. Everything emanates from the existence of this primordial force-God.

Our belief systems must be linked to desire of knowing God, the supreme for enlightenment. The human mind is designed to directly communicate with our Supreme by placing our desire before Him. As we are born, we are plugged into the Divine matrix and its consciousness is transferred. Science cannot solve the ultimate mystery of nature as we are part of the same mystery that we are trying to solve. Our conscious matrix tries to make sense out of everything and our concept of God is the highest concept in our mind. Scientists working on String Theory have been developing a new theory, which points to the existence of God, or an intelligent designer for the universe. We think that we are the body, and we are the mind, but in reality we are the spirit.

It is inevitable to regain our experience of connectedness with the entire web of life. When life is broken down into thoughts, concepts, and beliefs, we cannot directly experience the unity of everything. The natural world is a community of plants, animals, and humans. The web of life is that all living organisms, plants, and animals alike are bound together in a vast system of interlinked and interdependent lives. Though we like to remain separate, we are not. Everything happens to us reflects upon nature, as well as everything that occurs in nature reflects upon us. We humans need to honour the web of life through a deeper connection with self, nature, and world. Embracing the web of life brings wholeness, an integration of the instinctual psyche with existence. We need to regain our experience regarded as capturing rightful place in the web of life, which can enhance the well-being of the earth and all living beings. We are part of a natural and social web of life that supports and sustains us. God is omni-competent and creation is a projection of his mind.

Interconnectedness today holds a key role in the field of new sciences. Physicists have come to realize that the universe is interconnected in much subtler ways than had once thought. Quantum interconnectedness proves that everything is connected by the foundation way in which the fabric of the universe is woven into matrix. Inseparable quantum interconnectedness of the whole universe is the fundamental reality and that relatively independently behaving parts are merely particular and contingent forms within the whole. Measuring the condition or state of a quantum particle like electron can instantly change the state of another electron at a distance. As we learn that the human being is part of this universal field of information and connected through our consciousness we realize that our thoughts and actions have an impact on the whole. The essential feature of quantum interconnectedness is that the whole universe is enfolded in everything, and that each thing is enfolded in the whole. The understanding of quantum science does enhance ideas about God.

The laws of nature which govern the universe, place on us the power and responsibility to synthesize our own sense of meaning. We want to achieve a simple understanding of nature, and the path to simplicity is nothing but unification. A beautiful theory of nature is one in which the connections invisibly arise. Everything fits together, and if we try to change even a tiny part, the whole edifice collapses. The desire for God and for a theory of the whole cosmos might have the same cause. Everything exists at once with its opposites. The universe fills us with a sense of beauty, wonder, and mystery. The cosmic spirit of beauty and harmony lends the term God. Human beings regard themselves as characters in a cosmic drama. The universe is unity with an interactively and genetically related community, bound together in an inseparable relationship in space and time. The more the universe seems comprehensible, the more it also seems pointless. We see God crafting in abundant complex universe that includes our life- giving home: the Earth.

CHAPTER SIX

Polar Opposites

The creator of the universe- God amazes us with his richly developed polarity. From macroscopic cosmos to the microcosm of quantum universe, each molecule in our body exhibits the same polar forces holding them together as is present in the interstellar reaches of outer space. The fundamental substance of the universe is a direct expression of the most primary duality. The concept of polarity is the essence of the underlying unity of the dualistic pairs. Through the concept of duality, we can see an endless interplay between an infinite set of polarities or polar opposites. All too often, we spend our days chasing the poles of the pair that attracts us and keeping away from the pole that repulses. Without the universal law of polarity, gravity, heat, and electricity would not have been possible. The principle of Yin/Yang describes that opposites coexist to create the balance of the universe. The universe depends on the duality of polarity. What we manifest is a combination of these polarities in varying degrees. We are the essence of the concept of polarity and a continuum of polarities exists within us.

The polarity of opposites simply implies that the purpose of the universe is equilibrium. Everything is dual; everything has poles; everything has its pair of poles. We can see a lot of polarities in the universe- things that are each other's opposites, but connected together. The law of duality or polarity works with all the universal principles. Eastern mysticism looks at the two cosmic energies/principles endlessly interacting with the one forever flowing and morphing into other. We live in a world of opposites, where gain and loss, good and bad, pleasure and pain, life and death are as inevitable as the twin sides of the same coin. Duality is an essential concept that must be grasped if one wants to have a deeper understanding of the universe. The principle of polarity embodies the truth that all manifest things have two sides, two aspects, and two poles. Ardhanariswara, a popular iconographic form in Indian culture conveys the unity of opposites in the universe. It symbolizes that the male and female principles are inseparable and signifies the totality that lies behind duality.

God who is always and forever the Creator of all that is in the universe has put polarities into ultimate reality. The principle of polarity states that everything in our universe is dual, that each concept has two poles and everything has its opposites. The existence of one side of the polarity directly implies the existence of the other side of the polarity: one could not exist without the other. Everything has a contrasting opposite, but the two halves work cohesively together to make a whole, just like the Yin/Tang symbol. In terms of physics the yin-principle embodies spatial aspects and the yang-principle embodies the time aspect. At the atomic level of matter, we find dual aspect- it appears as particle and as wave. In some situations the particle aspect is in dominance, in other aspects the particle behaves more like a wave. The idea that all opposites are polar and they will always be a manifestation of the interplay between the two sides is the essence of all Eastern traditions. The unity of all opposites becomes a vivid expression in Zen words.

Things in nature appear in paired opposites depend on each other to complete a function or create a whole. Everything is polarized, whether in the visible universe or in the invisible forces of life itself. Metaphysical examples of the duality are the North Pole and South Pole of a magnet, the male and the female bioforms, the positive and negative electric charge etc. The attraction and repulsion generated by the two oppositely charged poles creates a flow of energy. The law of polarity says that everything in the universe has an opposite to and it is equal. The dual nature is also exhibited by light- it is emitted and absorbed in the form of protons, while travel through space it appears vibrating electric and magnetic field. The dual nature of matter and radiation is indeed most startling. The opposites are simply different manifestations of the same thing. It is the very existence these two opposites that allow us to understand life. Polarity manifests itself on the mental plane, which is activated as per the will, wish, and ignorance of the individual.

God has designed the physical world with polarities. Our opposing values are both integral aspects of a whole. The Tao suggests that we find oneness and unity within these paradoxes and acceptance of both sides. Metaphysically the entire universe is based on the duality. North and South are two polarities that co-create a torsion field around a planet. The duality aspect reveals the potential in all things and the polarity aspect creates the solution. The polarity and the duality provide insights into all the aspects of the whole. There are two sides or aspects of all things- people, situations, circumstances, and experiences. The particle picture and the wave picture are considered as two complementary descriptions of the same reality. Things that appear as opposites are in fact only two extremes of the same thing in our lives. Every emotion and every feeling has two sides. To live a peaceful life we need to be aware about duality paradoxical unity in day to day life. We need to accept the negatives of life, because without negative we cannot enjoy the positive.

No matter what we experience, there will always be an opposite, which is the make- up of nature. Both the static and dynamic forces are present in existence, in nature, and in the universe. Everything can be separated into two wholly opposite parts, and that each of those still contain the potentiality of the other. Duality is the two sidedness and polar complement of the world we live in. Duality teaches us that every aspect of life is created from a balanced interaction of opposite and competing forces. These opposing forces merely balance each other like the dual wings of the bird. The law of polarity is universal and it operates without our knowledge. For anything to exist for us at all, it needs an opposite to compare it with, or it will remain non-existent to our consciousness. Neither Yin nor Yang can stand alone: each is necessary to the existence. The law of polarity is about keeping the energy flowing in the right direction, similar to how the energy flows in the battery. We know that for every action there is an equal and opposite reaction.

All manifested things created by God have two sides, or two aspects, or two poles. Eastern philosophies point to Yin and Yang with the idea that there are two opposites that together make a complete circle. Geometric patterns and designs not only symbolize the universe's structure and nature, process, and symmetries, conflicts, and oppositions. The nature of the world's substance is paradoxical and its process is dialectical. Only when we integrate both sides of polarity, we will truly find our true selves. There is nothing in the universe, which is not subject to polarity and their interaction. Understanding the law of polarity helps us see both sides of a person, situation, or circumstance. Each physical atom not only in the human body, but of all physical matter contains positive and negative charged elements. Positrons, electrons, and neutrons create the balance that holds a single atomic molecule together. The physical and metaphysical aspects inherent in the energy of the universe that surrounds us are where the polarity begins.

Everything blends to form unique and vibrant combinations of polarity. The power generated by opposites yet has the essence of each opposite held within it. The opposites are simply different manifestations of the same thing. Like and unlike are the same, opposites are identical in nature. No matter how right we are about something, there will be a situation where we will be proven wrong. We embrace the wave of the universe in the polar vibration and in the wave of opposites. We each make it negative or positive by how we choose to think about it. We can feel the polarity in relation to people we meet, and we feel a pull or repulsion. The law of polarity helps us apply it and align ourselves with it to transform the way we think. We can suppress and transform undesirable thoughts by concentrating on the opposite pole. All truths are but half truths, and every truth is half false, as there are two sides to everything. The horse shoe theory suggests that when we look at far-left and far-right ideologies they are opposites though are identical in nature.

The concept of duality and polarity encompass all things in the universe. There are two poles or opposites, and the difference between the two extremes of one thing is called polarity. Polarity is essentially the glue in the bio-mechanics of physical matter. The duality inherent in nature serves to produce energetic interactions. This is witnessed in the interactions of positrons and electrons within the atomic structure. Magnetic fields display positive and negative polarities. We cannot have a left without right, an up without a down, a failure without a success, and a good without a bad and so on. Thoughts themselves have a polarity, which allows a person to shift his thinking along the continuum between the extremes. Force and matte, particles and waves, motion and rest, existence and non-existence- these are some of the opposite or contradictory concepts which are transcended in modern physics. Faced with a reality which lies beyond opposite concepts, physicists and mystics have to adopt a special way of thinking. One of the principle polarities in life is the one between the male and female sides of nature.

The notion of dynamic balance is essential to the way in which the unity of opposites is experienced in Eastern mysticism. Space and time themselves are two concepts which seems entirely different, but have been unified in relativistic physics. The law of polarity calls for change, and as humans we do not like to change by nature. Everything transforms and changes all the time. Polarity is part of the very transformation and creation going on in our universe. The crux of the law of polarity is to teach us that with every failure lies a possibility of success. The dual nature of light is expressed as the wave nature of particle and the particle nature of wave. Polarity is also defined as the possession or manifestation of two opposing attributes, tendencies, or principles. Polarity is an essential condition for existence, for without it, a physical universe could not exist. Everything we can experience or we cannot experience has equal opposites available in the universe. God created the polar opposites to coexist in order to create the balance of the universe.

CHAPTER SEVEN

Fine-Tuning

The universe must be so perfectly structured for us to exist- it is called fine-tuning, which cries out for explanation leading to teleological argument for God. Evidence of fine-tuning is recognized by all physicists and astronomers of all religions and philosophies. Scientists of all worldview agree that the physical constituents of our universe and the conditions of the early universe are exquisitely fine-tuned for life. The universe is able to support life, which deliberately depends on various fundamental characteristics, notably in the form of the law of nature, and notably in the values of some constants of nature, and on aspects of the universe. Physical constant is a fundamental invariant quantity observed in nature and appearing in the basic theoretical equations of physics. It turns out that it takes 26 dimensionless constants to describe the universe as simply and completely as possible. In order for life to arise in the universe, a series functional physical constants must take values that allow for large structures to be formed.

The universe really was born with a perfect balance between all the stuff in it, and the initial expansion rate. It is possible that we see the universe the way we see it today, because this balance has been caused by God. Our universe has several properties that are set to precise values, and slight changes to those values would prevent life as we know it. When the Big Bang occurred billions of years ago, the matter in the universe was uniformly distributed. There were no galaxies, or stars, or planets- just particles floating about in the dark void of space. As the universe expanded outwards from the Big Bng, gravity pulled ever-so-quietly on the matter, gathering into clumps that eventually became stars, galaxies, and planets. But the gravity had to have just the right force. If it was a bit stronger, it would have pulled all the atoms together into one big ball. This would have ended quickly into one Big Crunch. And if gravity was a bit weaker, the expanding universe would have distributed the atoms so widely that they would never have been gathered into stars and galaxies.

The fine-tuning is the proof of God existence, but the existence of God is not a scientific question. Life as we know it would be impossible if any one of several physical constants had slightly different values. Most people are curious to figure out why the universe is the way it is both scientifically and theologically. When most people hear the idea of a fundamental constant, they think about the constants of nature that are inherent in our reality. We do not know why does our universe possess a perfect symmetry with respect to charge, but a slight asymmetry with respect to matter and anti-matter. What is really spooky is that even tiny changes in most of the physical constant tend to make life and even the universe as we know it impossible. The fundamental laws of physics we presently understand them depend on about 26 parameters. The numerical values of the physical constants depend on the system of units in which they are expressed. The world we see around seems to be rooted in scientific laws. But the fundamental constants are the gods of modernity.

We cannot ignore the fact that to many the fact that the universe is fine-tuned for intelligent life shows the hand of the Creator God. When we think about our universe at a fundamental level, we think about all the particles in it and all the forces and interactions that occur between them. Agnostics wonder how surprising it is that the laws of nature and the initial condition of the universe should allow for the existence of beings who could observe it. Scientists also have found that even if the multi-verse models are right, the multi-verse would not eliminate fine-tuning. Despite the delusion of creationists, evolution by natural selection, currently gives us the most elegant, fulfilling and scientifically-grounded explanations as to how the complexities of the natural world developed. The basic idea is that the features must fall in turn a very narrow range of possible values for chemical- based life to be possible. The universe is really fine-tuned, and our existence is all the proof we need. In other words, we are unarguably fine-tuned to the universe we find ourselves.

The curious things about these physical constants are that they seem to float relatively free of the fundamental laws of physics, and they have the values they do.If we want to know why the universe is as it is, we need to know why of all the possibilities, ours is the actual universe. The cosmic constants include: gravitational force constant, electromagnetic force constant, strong nuclear force constant, weak nuclear force constant, and cosmological constant. The initial Brute Facts include; initial distribution of mass energy, ratio of masses for protons and electrons, velocity of light, and mass excess of neutron over proton. The charge on the electron is a fundamental property of a physical particle: it is the smallest unit of electric charge found free in nature. The universal gravitational constant relates the magnitude of the gravitational attractive force between two bodies to their masses and the distance between them. If we know the laws of physics- gravitation, quantum mechanics, electromagnetism, nuclear forces etc- all we need are the relationships that tell us by how much.

A fundamental physical constant is a physical quantity that is generally believed to be both universal in nature, and have constant value. The physical constants are the same in distant galaxies as they are here. Our universe is an intricate amazing place, and yet our greatest hopes of a unified theory- a theory of everything- out to decrease the number of fundamental constants we need. But the more we learn about the universe, the more parameters we are learning it takes to fully describe it. We should very strongly expect that a universe in which constants, laws, and conditions formed mindlessly and purposelessly, would be one in which life was almost certainly impossible. A cosmic intelligence seems to have fine-tuned our universe at its beginning to evolve stable galaxies, life, and mind. The quantum source for dark energy, often referred to as a cosmological constant is a true puzzle. Science now faces the question of why the universe appears to have been fine-tuned to allow the appearance of complex life- a question that has some potentially uncomfortable answer-a superpower.

Theory and equations that are absolute and universal, have centrally fundamental physical constants-the speed of light, the mass of a proton, the constant of gravitational attraction. Although our physical theories give us a powerful understanding of the universe, they do not explain physical constants. Every universal constant lays at the heart of physical sciences, since these constants are rooted in physical properties, which are generally thought they cannot change over space and time. Every electron has the same charge, whether they are here on Earth, or in a galaxy billions of light years away. Also the charge they have now should be the same charge they had at the dawn of time. Wherever we are in the universe, the mass of the electron, the speed of light, and the strength of gravitational force is the same. We plug these fundamental constants so often into our equations and calculate the properties of matter and energy. These constants pose a mystery- why do they have the values they do? Arguably God has intentionally fine-tuned these constants.

There is also the fine-tuned level of dark energy which we know very little about this mysterious substance that fills the universe. The teleological argument on the life, the universe, and everything in existence tell us about the fine-tuner God. This seems to be a much better and more consistent explanation than chance or necessity. A universe with too much matter and energy for its expansion rate will collapse in short order, while a universe with too little will expand into oblivion before it is possible to even form atoms. But our universe neither collapsed nor failed to yield atoms after the Big Bang, possibly because those two sides of the equation appears to be perfectly balanced. Whenever we run into an unexplained phenomenon it is our duty to seek our explanation. The term fine-tuning is used to characterize sensitive dependence of facts or properties on the value of certain parameters. All our mathematical and physical theories are built upon certain constants in nature. There are 26 fundamental constants in total, and these are dimensionless, meaning they are abstract number values.

The different combinations of the physical constants are strange, but still capable of supporting highly complicated systems and possible life. Why does the mathematical structure underlying the universe allow life to form? God is also value operator of a particle field known to some as the light in the tunnel. Whenever we examine the universe in a scientific manner, there are a few assumptions that we take for granted as we go about our investigation. We assume that the fundamental constants, properties, and laws associated with the material universe do not spontaneously change. If the fundamental constants are identical at all times and laces, the universe should show us that atoms behave the same everywhere we look. The fundamental constants of physics, such as the velocity of light, the Planck's constant, the charge, and the mass of the electron, and so on provide for us a set of absolute units for measurement of distance, time, mass etc. A supernatural power has provided a mechanism for creating these conditions that appear to be fine-tuned to us.

The contents of nature have been surrounded by mystique, and without them the laws of physics are sterile. When scientists quantify their observations, the laws of nature seem to follow a certain set of numerical values that seen consistent across space and time. These values are known as physical constants and they appear to provide symmetry across the universe. The laws of physics written in the language of mathematics, allows us to calculate how things interact through the forces of the universe. Within this mathematics lies he constants of nature-numbers that determine the physics of the universe. The existence of God can be explained by the fine-tuning phenomenon. A common sense interpretation of the facts suggests that a super-intelligence has been the real cause. Even the multi-verse universe model would not and could not replace God. Fundamental constants are believed to hold all around the universe, and each of these are fine-tuned by the Creator God. Scientific explanations cannot replace God, but rather increase our wonder and praise of the Creator God.

CHAPTER EIGHT

Clockwork Universe

Clockwork universe refers to the concept of the universe as a system that behaves in a manner as patterned and dependable as a mechanical clock. The myth of clockwork universe is one of the most persistent and pervasive myths in the history of science. We behold the heavens moving with a prodigious celerity, and causing an annual succession of the different seasons of the year, which vivify and preserve all things shows the world is directed. The regular motions exhibited by the sun, moon, and planets provided the basis for elaborate medieval clocks that could mimic the patterned motion of these celestial objects. Given the way mathematics works in the universe, our universe observes a whole bunch of laws of physics and other possible laws of physics seem equally likely. The entire cosmos, from quantum particles to the formation of galaxies, is a perpetual runtime flowing from simple rules. The spooky nature of material things shows that the world is incorporeal- a realm built out of wavicles of quantum probabilities. Ancients firmly believed in an eternal, all-powerful, and all-knowing God.

In the theological contexts, the clockwork analogy has two essential features: God as creator of the clockwork, and God as sustainer of the clockwork. Spin is ubiquitous in the cosmos. Particles rotate as do stars and galaxies. This comes about simply from conservation of angular momentum. The earth spins. The planets spin. Even the sun spins. All this spinning could not just be coincidence. In our cosmic backyard everything we see spins, rotates, and revolves in some fashion or other. Why does everything in the universe spin? As gases of varying densities moved around space, a triggering event caused these gases to coalesce. As the gravity of these bodies increased, they began pulling in everything around them, causing these bodies to spin. A curious phenomenon here is that, the spin appears to move in the same direction: counter- clockwise: Venus is the planet that seems to to be spinning clock-wise, and astronomers are not quite sure why. Regardless of whether it spins clockwise or counter-clockwise, everything in the universe moves and spins from small asteroids to entire galaxies.

Our universe is an amazing machine that consists of a number of integrated parts which function harmoniously, presumably for the accomplishment some purpose. The universe around us is made of systems that each have processes to fulfil everyday and each system is surrounded by an environment. There are inexplicable links between spin directions of galaxies and the structure formed by these links. All bodies rotate on their axes in the counter-clockwise direction, and this ensures order in the movement of bodies to avoid chaos. Why everything in the universe is spinning? How spin is generated. That is a really hard question to solve. It is an unsolved question in cosmology. We understand the motion of the planets under the influence of gravity, without knowing the cause of gravity. There is one idea that the universe runs on a grid of cellular automata. Cellular automata would extend to include everything and may be the universe itself is nothing, but a great cellular automata. The whole thing is run by a supernatural power called God. God is the ultimate software and source code.

The universe could be thought of as a great machine, acting according to fixed laws and God as a clockmaker. In the philosophy of clockwork, we need to understand the frame of a clock, and the dependence of the wheels upon one another, without knowing the cause of the gravity. The balance that keeps the planets adjusted correctly in their relationship to the sun is truly astounding. New research suggests the universe is teaching itself physics as it evolves, and the learning of the universe in similar to evolution. Our earth rotates on its axis daily and revolves around the sun annually. The earth rotates on its axis relative to the sun every 24.0 hours mean solar time, with an inclination of 23.45 degrees from the plane of its orbit around the sun. The earth's orbit is elliptical. The spin of the bodies is the most important fundamental property of matter and one that is essential for the celestial body motion mechanics and the proper functioning of the universe. All astronomical objects, including black holes are formed by gravity pulling matter together.

The idea of clockwork universe sees the world functioning like a mechanical clock wound up by God, ticking with precision, it gears controlled by the law of physics. Space is the sensorium of God with direct divine action of all forces for order and vitality. There is an idea that the universe is run by simulation, and the new science of digitization says that the universe itself is the ultimate computer. Physics is like a software program, and the entire universe sounds like a simulation of physics. Scientists predict the existence of anti-matter, but no reason has ever been given why the matter inherently needs an inverse of the same mass but opposite charge. It is of significant interest that the sun along with its planets-family is travelling in a gigantic orbit within the Milky Galaxy. When things collapse under their own gravity in space, any small amount of asymmetry in the collapse will be enough start it spinning. The fine tuning that is to be seen in physics and cosmology, and the unreasonable effectiveness of mathematics in the natural sciences is belief in a sovereign creator God.

The conception of the universe as a huge regulated and uniform machine that operates according to natural laws in absolute space, time, and motion shows that God is a master builder. Foremost among the findings is that along with gravity, matter at all levels exhibits axial spin. All congregations of matter spin on their own axis in the counter-clockwise direction. This inherent property of matter to spin on its axis is what initiates all celestial body motions and makes such motions perpetual. The constant motion of the heavens, the regular courses of the stars, the agreeable proportion and connection of all things attribute to an intelligent cause. The universe is thought of as something both designed and conceptualized by a divine artificer. God is the Prime Mover who brought into being the world in its lawfulness, regularity, and beauty. Many of nature's mysteries come in questions such as why does space have three dimensions? Why are there three fundamental constants in nature? Why do black holes have only three properties- mass, charge, and spin?

The most famous appeal to God as the designer and maker of the universe is especially in relation to its biological aspects. Through theological belief, we understand the laws of nature are constant and regular, and for ought we know, all of them may be resolved into one general and extensive power. The universe is full of spin, from the micro whirl of a molecule to the epic revolution of a galaxy. There is possible connection between the motions of galaxies and the wider cosmic web. The sun spins under its own inertia and does not need any help to keep it going. From our tiny human perspective, our planet is a rotating orb, located in a solar system that sweeps around the centre of the Milky Way, which is itself just one of billions of spinning galaxies across the observable universe. If earth stops spinning all at once, it will be enormously catastrophic for much of the planet's surface. Rotational inertia is a property of any object that can be rotated. The law of angular momentum dictates that everything in a system rotates in the same direction.

Natural philosophers see the universe as a vast machine operating by mechanical laws of interaction between particles. Our planets have continued spinning because of inertia. In the vacuum of space, spinning objects maintain their momentum and direction- their spin- because no external forces have been applied to stop them. Even the tiniest amount of rotational motion can have an astronomical effect on the movement of celestial bodies. New researchers would like to observe the universe at the intersection of theoretical physics, computer science, and philosophy. Scientists have discovered numerous physical laws and constants with fixed values to define the universe. The time travelling nature of the universe allows astronomers to observe galaxy evolution over time. The architecture of the universe with the just proportion of all parts indicates the traces of the divinity or the seal of God. It is a single vision of the cosmos as a whole that contains both matter and spirit that involves both nature and the superintendence of God.

The clockwork metaphor is used to argue for both divine transcendence and the radical contingency of creation. A remarkable feature of this great machine is the precision with which its integral parts work. The central features of theological conception of the world- the role of super-mechanical forces, the reality of processes of degeneration in the cosmos, is due to omnipresence of God. Scientific discoveries of the twentieth century have opened the doors for a renewed look at intelligent design evidences concerning the existence of God. Even famous ancient philosophers postulated that the world as an illusion rather than the reality. Hinduism aptly considers the entire creation as God's play. Buddhism emphatically says the world is an illusion. There is a kind of religious element to the notion of a giant simulation, a sense that there is a higher and purer reality. It is believed that God placed the planets at different distances from the sun so that each one might, according to the degree of its density, enjoy a greater or smaller amount of heat from the sun.

Many thinkers believe in the existence of God- like forces outside of the continuum. The ancients treat them with reverence, believing that they are responsible for the patterns of coincidence and serendipity within the universe. The physical ordering of the created order is the clear evidence of God's most wise and excellent contrivances of things. God sits enthralled at the centre of creation and is a participant in the world, not a spectator. God not only composes or puts things together, but is himself the author and preserver of their original forces or moving powers. It is most natural to suppose God to be the chief mover throughout the whole universe, and all other causes are dependent upon Him. The coherence and harmonious nature of the universe point to the origins in the eternal mind of God. The existence of God is proven by the laws of nature. God's glory should be considered in the amazing mechanics of the heavenly objects with stunning accuracy. God could be thought of as a divine clockmaker, who had constructed a particularly elegant piece of machinery.

CHAPTER NINE

Cosmic Dance

The Cosmic Dance represents the movement of the universe, from the galaxies and planets to all life to subatomic particles. Twentieth century subatomic world explorations show us that matter is intrinsically dynamic in nature. It means that subatomic particles do not merely exist as isolated entities, but as dynamic patterns. They form a network of interaction increasingly going on at the subatomic level. Every interaction involves a flow of energy, which manifests itself as the exchange of particles. Endless energy patterns are created as particles are created and destroyed in these interactions. On a visible level these interactions and particles give rise to stable structures, which build up the visible material world. Again they do not remain static, being made up of particles dynamic in nature, and have an observable order and rhythm in the patterns. Thus, from a scientific standpoint, we can ascertain that the whole universe is in a constant state of motion or activity, a continuous Cosmic Dance of energy. This is what we understand about the Cosmic Dance of Siva.

The Cosmic Dance features the parallels between modern quantum physics, astrophysics and ages-old spiritual wisdom. The symbolism of Siva is religious, art, and science merged as one In God's endless dance of creation, preservation, and destruction is hidden a deep understanding of the universe. The form of Siva in Cosmic Dance is one of the most iconic and perhaps even a stereotypical representation of classical Indian culture. According to Hindu mythology, Siva is the Cosmic dancer, who performs his divine dance to continue the unfolding of all existence, and create harmony in the universe. For the modern physicist Siva's dance is the dance of subatomic particles, the basis of all existence and of all natural phenomena. Modern physics has shown that the rhythm of creation and destruction is not only manifest in the turn of seasons and in birth and death of all living creatures, but is also the very essence of inorganic matter. The whole thing is there in the dance of Siva- the world of space and time, matter and energy, creation and destruction, and the world of psychology.

The Cosmic Dance aims to help us embrace our life as an open-ended adventure that is part of an open-ended and, spontaneity -filled Cosmic Dance. The figure and iconography of Nataraja captured the imagination of veritable thinkers of the world. A metaphor is drawn between the Cosmic Dance of Siva and the modern study of the Cosmic Dance of subatomic particles. It is a cosmic symbol, which is both cosmic, psychological, and spiritual. Though the galaxies appear to be locked in a Cosmic Dance, they are separated by tens of millions of light years. At a fundamental level of particles, there is no separation between us and what is outside us. The dance of Siva is the clearest image of the activity of God, which any art or religion can boast of. The dance of Siva symbolizes that the manifold forms in the world are not fundamental, but illusory and ever changing. The scientific symbolism of

Nataraja statue is the phenomena taking place within each of us at the atomic level and at this very moment. Siva's dance beats create the designs and the design is the symbol of the universe.

The Cosmic Dance creates endless energy patterns as particles are created and destroyed in these interactions. Siva is the personification of the divine universe, and the Cosmic Dance of Siva would mean the ceaseless change and flow of energy throughout the universe from the microcosm to the macrocosm. As for the physicists, even they began to talk about God, once they gained a greater understanding of the universe. The Nataraja idol validates the two grand themes of modern physics- the fundamental unity, and the intrinsically dynamic nature of its natural phenomenon. What appears as creation and destruction is only a transformation from one form to another in accordance with physical laws. According to the quantum field theory, the dance of creation and destruction is the basis of the very existence of matter. The subatomic particles do not merely exist as isolated entities, but as a dynamic pattern. The most fundamental laws of physics are: conservation laws, conservation of mass, conservation of energy, and conservation of momentum.

The Cosmic Dance phenomena in nature are the results of this Cosmic Dance between energized particles and the forces of gravity, electromagnetism, strong and weak nuclear forces. In 2004, the government of India gifted the European Organization for Nuclear Research or CERN, a 2-meter tall Nataraja statue, which now stands at the entrance of the facility in Switzerland, where the world's most powerful particle accelerator is installed. All scientific equations are mathematical representations or precise quantification of the action between particles and forces.

Mathematical equations are the notation of the choreography of the Cosmic Dance- the choreographers are the physical laws of nature. Life is a Cosmic Dance, The Cosmic Dance is not random motion, but is beautifully choreographed and the movements obey laws of nature. it is as if every particle in nature is reaching out to every other particle and engaging in a beautiful Cosmic Dance. All forms are made of the same building blocks, which are connected and interact through forces.

The Cosmic Dance is the harmony existing between systems that are so strongly interdependent that they behave like a single entity. Quantum entanglement says that particles on opposite sides of the universe can be intrinsically linked so that they share information instantly. Dark Matter is the mysterious substance in space that provides the cosmic foundation for the entire structure in the universe. The Cosmic Dance of Siva is so incredible that its vibrations give rise to the world, and is the reason behind the appearance of everything. Siva as Nataraja represents apocalypse and creation as he dances away the illusory world of maya transforming it into power and enlightenment. The Cosmic Dance is very ancient, representing the Eastern mystic's dynamic view of the universe. For sheer rhythmic movement, delicacy of contour lines, and limped grace in form and texture, there is nothing to approach the dancing icon of Nataraja. The philosophical, spiritual, and cosmic interpretation of Nataraja has their main root idea behind- the manifestation of primal rhythmic energy.

The Cosmic Dance of Siva is said to have been performed in Chidambaram in Tamilnadu, a place that is identified with both the centre of the universe and the human heart. Chidambaram is the only temple where Siva is worshipped in a human form at the sanctum- Perhaps the most iconic of all dance symbols in Indian mythology. This image of Nataraja can be liked to a kind of premonition of modern astronomical ideas. The symbolic abstraction of this figure as it dances in the cosmic weightlessness state of change imparts a supernatural quality. Modern physics shows us that every subatomic particle not only performs an energy dance, but also is an energy dance itself- a pulsating process of creation and destruction. When individual subatomic particles are smashed against each other in high energy experiments, they do not scatter into smaller bits, instead they merely rearrange themselves to form new particles, using kinetic energy. Scholars around the world are enamoured of Nataraja- all embracing material world, with its flames, within this Siva's Cosmic Dance and is everywhere in the universe.

The Cosmic Dance of Siva is that which pervades and permeates every particle of the creation. According to quantum field theory, each and every subatomic particle resonates, dances, and emits the energy. Lord Siva is the personification and representation of the divine knowledge and supreme underlying intelligence. Siva is seen dancing in sheer abandon, hair locks wildly swaying and his limbs placed in broad symmetry. Siva is seen creating a very delicate balance between existence and non-existence. He stands beautifully balanced on his right leg, trampling a tiny figurine, while the entire scene is framed by a circle of flames. The dwarf demon at his feet represents the evils of ignorance and ego. The four hands represent the rhythm of unity of life- upper hand holds a drum to symbolize the primal sound of OM and left hand holds a flame to symbolize the destruction. His lower right hand shows that he bestows protection on the universe. To understand the true nature of the cosmos, one must unite Siva's creative energy and cosmic consciousness.

The Cosmic Dance of Siva represents the five acts- the birth of the world, its maintenance, its destruction, the soul's obscuration, and liberation. The entire universe and all life are connected: matter and spirit are not separated and divine energy reigns in all of us. Nataraja has become an icon, not just of Indian culture, but even of science progress and of a world beyond. Siva's frenzy is seen as a metaphor for the flux of the subatomic, or God particles being observed by CERN physicists. The trouble is that quantum physics seems to defy the common-sense notions of causality, locality, and realism. Quantum mechanics is weird, the theory, which describes the workings of tiny particles and forces. Neuroscientists are astonished to find that the brain circuit for spirituality is centred in one of the most evolutionary preserved structures in the brain. The spirituality in general and religiosity in particular is an off shoot of our brain's main function: creating meaning. Nataraja reminds us that all of nature dances in cyclic manner, where there is neither beginning nor end.

The Cosmic Dance of Siva is the dancing universe; the ceaseless flow of energy going through an infinite variety of patterns that melt into one another. Nataraja's dance conveys meaning through attributes such as postures and gestures with symbolic elements. His dance is the manifestation of the world called his play. We ourselves are a mere collection of fundamental particles of the universe. Many of the particles that make up those cells have actually existed for millions of millennia. We are not this solid substantially looking mass, but instead we are empty space in which particles in motion. We are primarily empty space and particles engaged in the Cosmic Dance. In this dance there is no separation between what is inside of us and what is outside. There is a cyclic movement, but nothing is ever in the same place. On a visible level these interactions and particles, give rise to stable structures which build up the visible material world. The making of the universe is Siva's Cosmic Dance that has coherence and the formation synchronizes to dance.

CHAPTER TEN

Conversing Universe

The universe always amazes us with its continuous flow of communication, giving us signs and symbols that so directly correlate to our individual circumstances. Our sixth sense or insights identify the signs and symbols as the messages from the universe. Intuition is the communication from the universe and that is voice inside us. Once we begin to recognize and engage with the signs and symbols around us, we have the power to see whatever we want to see. If we pay attention to what we see, or what we come into contact with, or signs and symbols from nature, we gain meaning to our lives. When we pay attention to any of the signs or symbols, and if they keep happening, it is a sure way to tell that the universe is trying to tell something. When we start to feel a lot more aligned and connected with the universe, we find more subtle and creative ways it sends us messages. Recognizing and receiving information through signs and symbols depends on our earnest seeking and just plain listening. Signs and symbols are not one size fit, we have to interpret them on an intuitive level.

The universe speaks to us all the time, but we do not always recognize the messages. Natural forces and universe conspire and communicate with us all the time. We just need to listen to them and interpret them carefully and understand accordingly. The more we pay attention to our heart's voice, the louder our mind begins to speak. There are many ways in which the universe communicates with us. The messages are delivered through nature, people, events, inner voice, things, and dreams. The universe communicates to us through dreams and our dreams are a mirror to the life we are living. Repetition, coincidence, and synchronicity are part of a personal conversation from the universe, intended to provide ease and guidance. When we call something in either consciously or subconsciously, then the universe will respond in the form of a reply or message of guidance on the path to manifesting our desires. The universe sometimes comes through some person to tell us a message is indeed miraculous. When we are tuned into how the universe communicates with us, our life becomes a lot less confusing.

The universe works in mysterious ways, and signs and symbols from the universe make available to us the tools, the resources, and the people. A synchronicity is a random occurrence of events that seem coincidental, serendipitous, and related, yet are not connected by any one thing. Universal spirit is in everything and everywhere, intertwined in the ordinary moments of life. Dreams are our nightly gurus, which help to iron out the kinks in our subconscious minds. Inspiration can come from the most unexpected places or insignificant places, when we visit them. Déjà vu happens and it is believed that it is a moment suspended in the now. When we set the intent, then all of a sudden, we meet a random person that can help us on our journey. Sometimes getting a text or phone call from someone or hearing a message can trigger a deep knowing inside us. A random idea or thought may pop into our head out of the blue, and out of nowhere. Most of the signs and symbols from the universe are repetitive and they show up until we get it right.

The universe communicates in subtle ways, but to hear the universe effectively, we want to relax and let our mind be open. Synchronicities are one of the most powerful ways that the universe communicates with us and we start experiencing them more and more as we start to awaken. Messages, guidance, and answers can come to us through our dreams. We need to look into the meaning of dreams to see what it can mean to us. We humans are dubbed as a tiny cell in a vast universe, actually contained in the entire universe within itself. We are not an isolated being, but connected to the universe in countless intricate ways. When we receive a message from a sign or symbol from nature, it deeply resonates with us and our inner truth gets awakened. Every sign or symbol that we get, we consider a miracle, because it is a direct connection with universe source. Repeated sightings of specific animals can be a message too, when we often see the same animal at the strangest or most needful times, we might see that as a sign that the universe is looking out for us.

The universe communicates through strange coincidences, repetitive numbers and words, objects, and endless other forms. Each number sequence can also have more specific meaning if we analyze what the numbers mean to us. Even seeing a certain pattern or sequence of numbers can provide hidden meanings. There is a pattern in each life waiting to be analyzed and interpreted. We are just in the universe as energy field that connects us to everything in nature. Let us listen to what the universe has to say to us, which can reveal a lot about reaching our goals and happiness. Meaningful coincidences are usually signs we are on the right path or Universal spirit comes to us in the form of people as the universe has a way of using people as vehicles to carry out certain messages. Synchronicity is a direct connection to the universal spirit and a sign that we are on the right path. These are all ways that the universal spirit is trying to tell us something and it is up to us to figure out what. Our intuition is our best helper and will probably throw a few hints that the universe may be trying to tell us.

The universe has given us the intuitive discernment to just know what a certain course of action to take. When we pick up signs and symbols, the universe is talking to us. We might brush them off at first thinking that is nothing, but something weirder happens that we cannot ignore. Number sequences are a beautiful way that higher selves communicate that we are alignment with the path we are currently on. Synchronicity is just a matter of recognizing that there is something way bigger happening behind the scenes and something way more profound that we can ever imagine. Each sign or symbol comes to us, has a message that is unique to us and to our specific situation. Through observation it helps us identify the signs or symbols easily and all we need to do is pay attention to those things. One of the top signs or symbols that the universe is talking to us is that a single dominant thought cuts through the mental fog and suddenly jolts us awake. The truth is whatever is happening in our life is for a reason, and there are no coincidences.

The universe we live in is alive and we are connected to it in the grand web of life. The signs or symbols we get are less ethereal and are sort of incorporated into the structures and routines of everyday life. This can be a random idea, a solution to a problem, or something we feel inspired to do. We pay attention to this and see what it can mean for us. The signals from our intuition, is just far quicker at picking up extrasensory clues than our conscious mind is. Part of the personal curriculum is the ability to decipher the often seemingly hidden signs, symbols, and messages through silent intuition. Countless people wish upon a star and attempt to project their request into the cosmos. The more we open ourselves to the powers that be, the easier it will be for us to find the answers we seek. The human body is a closed open system that is continually forming a communication between human genes and the universe. There is a divine order and timing to everything, and let us not forget that we are universal spirit, which is the essence of who we are.

The universe has different ways to send us signs and guidance, an we only need to know how to recognize them. It communicates with us naturally, through situations, people, and signs. We live and learn through the communicating universe directly via the instant wireless connection-the intuition. We need to learn to pay attention to signals and messages, and understand that God speaks to us every moment The signs or symbols are subtle, indirect, and can be gentle and quite, although sometimes pretty loud, and obvious too. Sometimes we are directed to meet a random person, who perhaps tells us something or does something that sparks something within us. We have to be present, open, and willing to receive answers as universal spirit tries to get our attention. We see signs at the place and time that we are meant to see them. The moment does not have to be glamorous for there to be a sign as we can get a sign even in the ordinary moments of life. If we want to become more powerful, we can start listening to the messages the universe is always sending us.

The universe expresses its intelligence in great simplicity and it is only our minds that try to know the why. When we understand how the universe communicates, the manifestation journey turns out to be filled with miracles. We are intrigued by the universe sometimes to go to some place or event to find answers to our questions. We are all spiritually connected and fundamentally one so that we have access to guidance. When we are in harmony with the universe, a higher consciousness brings the right things into our life. When ur desires are manifesting, we are feeling connected and aligned with a sense of flow in our life. This is also a sign that we are aligned with our truth and that we are on the right path. There is a co-creative universal intelligence, who is very much involved and continually seeking a dialogue. There is always a higher at play from whom we wait for signs. Whatever that keeps on placing itself in our awareness is something to be acknowledged because it holds powerful clues. We need to build a perfect relationship with the universe with a proper state of mind.

The universe is nothing other than our higher selves, our inner spirit, and our faith. The divine is eternal source of all abundance and guidance is always a manifestation of the divine. The divine seamlessly flows within and without us, constantly trying to catch our attention and guide our decisions. All we have to do is listen from a deeper spot within us and let the miracle unfold. It is in our inner stillness and silence that we will decipher the meaning and listen to the wisdom of the cosmos. Everything happens when it is meant to, and it is actually a blessing in disguise, though they seem like delaying our progress. The universe is providing a delay in order to stick to the perfect schedule of divine timing. Every adversity in our life carries an equal seed of opportunity and eventually we understand what the purpose of that occurrence. Often times when everything in our life falls apart, it is an invitation to learn to let go, and learn to detach from the world of form or it is an opportunity to awaken. The universe as God or super power hears and replies every time we ask.

CHAPTER ELEVEN

Beyond Science

Science cannot adjudicate over the existence or non-existence of God, because the domain of science is nature. Why did everything we need in order to exist come into being? For many physicists throughout history- people like Copernicus, Galileo, Newton- God was an inspiration in their scientific work. The observable physical world of material reality in which we live, is a secondary derivative. The natural world cannot contradict scripture or cannot speak against God. Figuring out how life began is both an exciting and a challenging scientific problem. Scientific hypotheses can be confirmed or disproved by evidence and liable for reframing. Science is an amazing, wonderful undertaking: it teaches us about life, the world, and the universe. Science's domain is to explore nature, while God's domain is in the spiritual world. New science has given a clear message: the world follows rules, rules that are fundamentally mathematical, the rules that humans can figure out. Science has also to come to function as meaning-making system in today's world.

Science and religion, considered as two independent and two distinct realms of inquiry, are now considered to be in dialogue. Truth is available to us through the avenues of both religion and science. People try to reconcile the claims of truths revealed by divine inspiration and those that are the product of earthly reason. Albert Einstein said the most beautiful thing we can experience is the mysterious. Science cannot examine or explain the purpose of the universe, which falls under theology or philosophy. God would never fade away from our hearts and minds, when we see into the secrets of the universe. Quantum mechanics allows us to think of special divine action. Ancient ideas about the non-material nature of a greater reality are being re-examined and re-envisioned today. Besides the world of material reality, there exists some other reality with another form of existence, which lies outside the realm of existence of the material world- that is the world of higher reality. Science speaks in the language of numbers, formulae, and discoveries about the ineffable harmonies of the all-wise God.

Twentieth century men and women are tempted to look upon science as a new God. It appears that there is a vast hidden wisdom or structure or knotty blueprint for even the most simple-looking element of nature. Francis Collins attempted to argue that the idea of God is compatible with Darwin's theory of evolution. He further added that he has found there is a wonderful harmony in the complimentary truths of science and faith. To most worshippers, a sense of the divine as an unseen presence is behind the visible world. For centuries the Vatican has appointed an astronomical observatory and has appointed a scientifically trained chief astronomer. Of course, religion lies closer to the heart of human nature and has a wider currency than science. Science and religion are consonant as regards the deepest of mysteries such as creation and consciousness. The insights that science brings to the deepest questions of the universe need to provide answer to the humankind's purpose. The world of higher reality is finite, eternal, and unchanging; where there is no time and space, motion, evolution etc.

Modern science has shaped a new earth and changed man's existence physically, socially, and intellectually. Creationists inevitably look for God in what science has not yet explained or in what they claim science cannot explain. All of the masses, charges, and forces of interaction in the universe had to be in just the precisely needed amounts so that early light atoms could form. Sir Francis Bacon believed in the existence of God, who was known as the founder of the scientific method. Biological evolution has not brought us the slightest understanding of how the first living organisms emerged from inanimate matter on this planet. Science has not revealed the highly complicated double-helix molecule, the life-propagating DNA would be formed. What is that allows humans to understand the mysteries of biology, physics, mathematics, engineering, and medicine? The deep human impulse is to understand the world, to know our place in it, and to marvel at the wonder of life and the infinite cosmos. What is that immense power of nature which has created one universe where everything is right?

Scientific exploration is inexorably moving deeper into intangible realms and will open new paradigm. Science is restricted to only providing naturalistic answers to explain what we see, but no hypothesis can include God. Scientists find inspiration beyond science- in a sense of reverence for the order of the universe and wonderment at its mysteries. Carl Sagan was open to the possibility that science would perhaps one day find compelling evidence to prove God. Science is the application of scientific observable concepts to the spiritual unobservable realm. The religious people believe that there is a great mystery, and we do not know what it is about in the universe. The majority of scientists are not atheists and any scientist who claims that science proves God does not exist is simply a poor scientist. We can look forward to a theory of everything, yet the question will always arise what explains that? Where does that come from? Science would always ask and answer empirical questions like what and how religion would confront the spiritual wondering why.

We live in an age when the results of science exercise the controlling influence in all walks of life. The way the universe exhibits ordered structure, which is open to science to investigate points to a mind behind it. By looking at order in the universe, we can infer purpose and from purpose, we begin to get some knowledge of the Creator-the planner of all. For some God is the abstract principle of harmony and order. Now scientific discoveries offer support to the spiritual as we find design and purpose behind the universe. Scientists now realize that the laws of nature must be incredibly fine-tuned to produce the universe we see. In the spooky quantum realm, the behaviour of particles is unpredictable. Many often feel that somehow intelligence must have been involved in the laws of the universe. Physicists have stumbled on signs that the cosmos is custom-made for life and consciousness. Maria Mitchell, a female astronomer was a religious seeker, who pursued a simpler sort of faith. We are challenged for an explanation of how a simple being could design a complex universe.

Science is no where near to explaining the deep mysteries of physics and cosmology. Why is our universe so precisely tailor-made for the emergence of life? Why are even tiniest particles of matter so unbelievably complicated? These questions have never been answered satisfactorily with a scientific solution. What we do know is that numerous physical constants are poised precisely at the magnitudes required to allow life to emerge. Most scientists do not become irreligious as a consequence of their becoming scientists. Eminent scientists of natural and mathematical sciences hold wide interest in reflection on God or religious faith or the spiritual value. The enormous usefulness of mathematics in the natural sciences is something bordering on the mysterious and there is no rational explanation for it. Why the nuclear fires inside stars giving us carbon, oxygen, nitrogen, iron, and all the other elements that are so essential for life to emerge? Scientists feel free to admire the complexity of the natural world, and praise it. Science is indeed discovered God and it did so as it unravelled the secrets of nature.

The more we study the creation through science, the more clearly we see that it must be the handwork of God. We are yet to know how Physical atoms and molecules can create something that exists in a separate domain that has no physical existence: human consciousness. Science has not revealed to us why the universe came into existence? What preceded its birth in the Big Bang? How all of things in the universe possible without some latent outside power to orchestrate the precise dance of elementary particles required for the creation of all the essentials of life? In science explanations are based on evidence drawn from observation of the natural world and experimentation. Yet science is a power tool for understanding and explaining the mechanisms and dynamics of the physical universe. Scientific theories change in the light of new discoveries, as what science has to say today may change tomorrow. We do not know where do symbolic thinking and self-awareness come from? For many scientists, the achievements of modern science offer support for spirituality and the very nature of God.

Physicists note that the more the universe has become comprehensible through cosmology, the more it seems pointless. They feel that there is a very deep fact about the universe: that our minds conform to the reality of the cosmos and we are somehow tuned to its truths. Few scientists abide by the miracles, and feel God can act without violating the laws of physics, while God selects which possibility becomes reality. Physicist's metaphorical use of the word God refers to the laws of nature as the mind of God. Some scientists believe in God, either as a prime mover, or as an active force in the universe. The more we know about the vast yet intricate and beautiful universe we live in, it is more awe-inspiring is the God who made it all. Scientists who allow their spirituality to be shaped by personal inquiry, gives them more potential to align with scientific thinking and reasoning. A few scientists maintain that understanding religious experiences within the context of science should in no way diminish their value. Normally God's domain must be examined with the heart, the mind, and the soul.

Science does not have the processes to prove or disprove the existence of God. Science can never prove or disprove the existence of God, because scientific ideas are provisional, capable of being overturned by evidence from experimentation and observation. Science can speak with authority in the realm of what the universe is made of, and why does it work this way? God's domain is in the spiritual world, a realm not possible to explore with the tools and language of science. From the microscope to the telescope God's creation is declaring his glory. Science is a gift from God, which helps us to try to glimpse God's mind and being to awe of it. It also means that we have now seen that science is the language that God used to speak us into being. Given that humans are finite, and constrained by language and culture, it is simply beyond our grasp fully to understand and articulate what God might signify? More than ever, God and science are needed to spark imagination about the many mysteries of the universe. Miracles are only the beginning of the ways in which we must reckon with God.

Author Bio

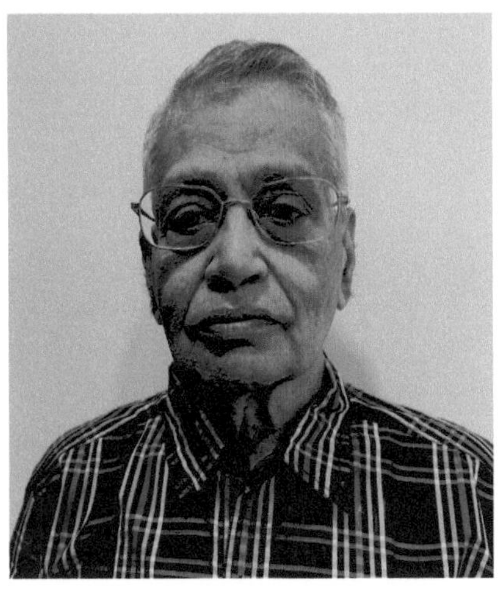

Prof. R V M Chokkalingam

Prof. RVM. Chokkalingam is a former lecturer/ curator/ scientist and now @ 78 is a local professor living in Bangalore, and is engaged in the study of existence of God in scientific terms. He is a science museum scholar, a science communicator, and a science writer. He has a lifetime contribution of 50 years in the public engagement with science. He has to his credit more than 160 articles in newspapers and magazines. He has authored around 20 books in science, philosophy, and nature. He is the recipient of Karnataka Government award for science communication in 2012. He is a paper airplane guy.

www.ingramcontent.com/pod-product-compliance
Ingram Content Group UK Ltd.
Pitfield, Milton Keynes, MK11 3LW, UK
UKHW040011200726
13854UKWH00001B/152

9 798885 464574